C000136499

# Preventing Suicide

*A Lay Person's Guide to Preventing Suicide*

# Preventing Suicide

*A Lay Person's Guide to Preventing Suicide*

## Susan Norman

Copyright © 2016 by Susan Norman.

ISBN:        Softcover        978-1-5245-0761-9
             eBook            978-1-5245-0760-2

All rights reserved. No part of this book may be reproduced or transmitted in any form or by any means, electronic or mechanical, including photocopying, recording, or by any information storage and retrieval system, without permission in writing from the copyright owner.

Any people depicted in stock imagery provided by Thinkstock are models, and such images are being used for illustrative purposes only.
Certain stock imagery © Thinkstock.

Print information available on the last page.

Rev. date: 06/14/2016

**To order additional copies of this book, contact:**
Xlibris
1-888-795-4274
www.Xlibris.com
Orders@Xlibris.com
743480

# Contents

**Part 1**
**Introduction 1**

**Part 2**
**Getting The Help You Need**

May 17, 2016

*Preventing Suicide by* Susan Jeanne Norman

*A Layperson's Guide to Preventing Suicide for Oneself and Loved One*

Dedication: This "workbook" is dedicated to Dr. Frances Perry, in Bowling Green, Ohio. She is the person that made me make "A Vow" which I delineate later. She saved my life when I needed to have it saved. God Bless her.

# Part 1

# Introduction 1

If you are presently immersed in suicidal ideation or thinking, get help immediately! This book has a lot of information intended to help you through this terrible situation but if you are already there, get help. Call a Crisis Line, Suicide Hotline, a doctor, or psychologist, a friend, parent, grandparent, someone in your life that you know cares about you. Ask for help and take it when they give it to you. You are worth it!

# Getting A Clue

What can we do as loved ones, family, neighbors, as a community to help people prevent suicide? Suicide numbers are up in certain groups, especially young people, the elderly, and increasingly our armed services personnel overseas. How can we be in the right place at the right time to help someone out of this terrible corner they have painted themselves into?

My heart has broken every time I have gone to a funeral or memorial service for someone I knew that took their own life. What could I have done? How could I be there for someone else before they reach the very end, give up to the demons within them?

In my heart of hearts I believe surely there is something that I could have done. I, for one, would have been happy to go and get the person and talked with them, taken them out for coffee at 2 a.m. to get him or her out of their own negative spiral downward.

So this "workbook" is written with love for those who may be in that dangerous place themselves or know someone else who is. To do something is better than doing nothing.

While the first and foremost goal of this book is to help you prevent suicide in yourself or someone else, once you have avoided suicide you must then get well again so that when things get bad for you again, as they are likely to do in everyone's life at some time or other, suicide is not an option, that you have real usable coping skills to get you through.

I am writing this book as a person who has avoided suicide for myself after two attempts when I was in my 20's and 30's. That has me pegged as a "high risk group". I am now 61 years old and have prevented myself from killing myself over thirty plus years.

I am not a licensed therapist, psychologist or psychiatrist. I believe that people in these professions are essential to preventing suicides and I encourage people to find a very good counselor that will help them. I have had two in my life that through working through serious issues in my life, have helped me avoid killing myself.

I am a lay person, who, by my definition, is a person who has experience and insight into this acutely painful issue in many people's lives, and may be able to share something helpful for you in your situation. I want to reiterate that I am not a licensed professional, and that should you need professional help you are encouraged to get it right away. Time is of the essence. Obsessing on suicide puts it forward in your mind and puts you at further risk. If you are in this space, get help immediately! You are worth it!

I did not do this on my own. I had a strong support network of friends, family and counselors over the years and all of them together have taught me how to hang on to life. So I have had a team of people that helped me. Start putting together your own team. These folks may save you when you need it most. Have them make an accountability pact with you and you make one with them. Write down or journalize your goals and how you will attain them.

I have lived through the suicides of some friends, acquaintances, and co-workers. My thoughts and experiences in the aftermath have always centered on "What could I have done for these people that others did not do?" "What could I have done?" As a proactive person, I believe there is something that can be done in terrible situations. The question is what is the best action for the circumstances? How can the suicidal person be treated with the greatest amount of respect possible in their process of protecting their life and moving on from there? This is a life and death situation and any person attempting suicide is by nature going to be scarred in some way by the experience. The key is to help them pick themselves back up and move on with their lives.

In this book I am going to set up some questions that you can journalize for yourself. I encourage you to take the time at the end of each chapter to discover where you or your loved ones are on these issues. These notes can be a starting point in discussions with a therapist of your choice.

I am writing to encourage you to not take your life and if you have someone in your life who is "at risk" to have some tools and ideas at hand to help you help them through this terrible time. While you may have heard of several things I am going to mention, I am trusting that this information may be new to someone who really needs it.

I want to impress on my readers, too, that this can be a time when you go deep inside yourself and bring up your most creative self to deal with potential suicide. The circumstances leading up to suicide can be as unique as the individual involved and the ways out of thinking about it, obsessing about it can be as creative as you are too. Your creativity can become a badge of honor, showing yourself and your loved ones your potential in working this problem out to ultimately prevent suicide. That is my hope and prayer for all of you, and my reason for sharing all of this.

Questions to journalize:

Where are you today on the question of suicide?

_____
_____
_____
_____
_____

Are you having suicidal ideation right now or in the recent past? Do you have a plan for committing suicide? Do you have a plan for preventing suicide? Your's or someone else's?

_____
_____
_____
_____
_____

What do you need to get out of reading this book?

_____
_____
_____
_____
_____

# Chapter 1

# Who I Am And Where I Am Coming From . . .

I think that people go through times in their lives when their life is threatened. Anything can set off a deepening spiral downward such as a loss of job, spouse, relationship, financial set backs and other life changing events. Some people manage to get through this time with skills they have and relationships they have developed, through their faith or other connections. But some people lose hope for their lives and then they begin to think things will never change and that they and others would be better off if they were dead.

I went through a long period of depression in my life. I had some life experiences that were, at times, seemingly hopeless.

I was born with a visible birth defect over my left eye. It was a tumor that was benign but grew slowly, that eventually destroyed my left eye which was exonerated in 1969, the summer before I entered high school.

When I was young people seemed to ask me all the time what was wrong with my eye. It made me feel ashamed and humiliated. I had no answer for them since it had always been with me. I spent years in doctors' and specialists' offices but there was little they could do.

In junior high school I spent days in class dreaming of cutting myself with razor blades. I never did actually cut myself until college but I would envision it daily. The removal of the tumor was a new start for me though I wore a black patch for 20 years following the surgery. The technology did not exist at the time for reconstructive surgery though

I would have that later. At the time it was enough to have the tumor gone so I could begin to live a more normal life.

But my life was far from "normal" in my teen years. I experienced a lot of bullying and harassment at school and after school. I believe I was rejected by many of my peers for being very different, for having something wrong with me. For years I planned my suicide in school and was blessed with some adults in my life that were a life line.

In junior high school there were several boys that harassed me almost daily, following me home after school, callin me names, sometimes kicking me. I have come to understand why young people kill people that are bullying them. I got them to stop but only after destroying some of their property. My mother went to their mothers and told them what was going on and for these boys to stop. They did eventually stop.

In high school I did not really have boy friends. So I became smart. National Honor Society smart. In high school I buried myself in my studies but my journals from those years show what a dangerous place I was in my head.

In college I attempted suicide for the first time, slitting my wrists in the dorm bathroom late one night after being rejected by the love of my life. I did not cut deep enough and so ended my attempt.

I dropped out of college several times and upon returning, I fell in love with a guy who would eventually reject me and I would attempt suicide a second time with pills. At that time friends forced me to start seeing a good counselor who brought me back to myself. A very good friend made me make a vow with her that if I ever got to the point where I was going to attempt to commit suicide again that I would get professional help.

Over the years I have had suicidal thoughts and ideation and have sought out professional help to get me out of where I was in my head. It was this vow with my friend that I believe saved my life for the rest of my life. More about this later.

Questions to journalize:

Who are you and where are you coming from?

---

---

---

---

---

What is your history with regard to suicide? Your attempts or the attempts of others.

---

---

---

---

---

Do you have a loved one that either committed suicide or has been in danger of doing so?

---

---

---

---

---

# Chapter 2

# Caring Adults

Much research has been done that shows that if a young person has one adult in their life that really cares about them, they will be able to ride out really tough times in their lives.

There are adults in this world that really care about young people and I had one of these people in my life growing up. Having one person that loved me unconditionally saved my life at that time. There was a period of time when my mother and I could not communicate with each other on a civil level, which is common for many teens. My friend's mother, GRACE, (never was a name more appropriate), would meet my friend and me at the back door of their home after school nearly every day. She would hug both of us but for me it was the only human touching I was receiving during many years. She stood about six feet tall and I was all of 4'10", quite round but diminutive. I literally looked up to her in a big way!

After the hug she would gather us up in her office area to one corner of their master bedroom. She would then talk to me and listen to me. Years later I wondered if she knew how close I was to killing myself so many times but she never said so. She just had this gift about her where she could listen to anyone talk about their life, not judging them under any circumstances. At this time of my life I envisioned long ribbons of blood running down my arms all during some of my more boring classes at school. There were times I could not stand to live any longer but somehow the daily routine was enough to keep me alive. There were many days when I asked myself if today would be the day when I would kill myself.

If you know a teen that needs to be listened to, you will never know how deeply this gift of yours may be appreciated for the rest of that person's life. You may never know that your conversations with this teen may have saved his or her life. Taking a small amount of time out with the teen and just listening to him or her can be life-saving. Growing up today is so difficult with so many expectations, concerns, worries, embarrassments and more that so many teens are stressed out to the max. The few minutes they spend with you may be just the stress reducer they need to face their daily lives.

Questions to Journalize:

Did you have an adult in your childhood or adolescence that loved you unconditionally who listened to you when you needed to be listened to?

--------------------------------------------------------
--------------------------------------------------------
--------------------------------------------------------
--------------------------------------------------------

What did you learn from that person that helped you grow up safely?

--------------------------------------------------------
--------------------------------------------------------
--------------------------------------------------------
--------------------------------------------------------

Do you have this kind of relationship with someone? A young person or someone else in your life?

--------------------------------------------------------
--------------------------------------------------------
--------------------------------------------------------
--------------------------------------------------------

How do you nurture this relationship? What more can you do to enhance this relationship?

--------------------------------------------------------
--------------------------------------------------------
--------------------------------------------------------
--------------------------------------------------------

Do you know a teen or young person that needs this from you? Is there anything that I holding you back?

--------------------------------------------------------
--------------------------------------------------------
--------------------------------------------------------
--------------------------------------------------------

# Chapter 3

## Deep Listening

I think it is this deep listening from human being to human being that is an essential key to affirming a person's life especially when they face suicidal ideation.

A man in my Adult Sunday School class killed himself at the height of his career. He appeared to have it all in life, a wonderful family, a great job, a new home and beloved friends, even a band he played in. So what was missing?

In retrospect I think that he did not have someone that was really listening to him or was saying and responding to him with only what they thought he wanted to hear. Everyone around him was extremely busy in their own lives. He had been on an anti-depressant from his physician and then another professional changed his meds. It was during this interim period when he killed himself. Everyone said it was the change in meds that threw him but I think he could not express what was going on inside of himself to the degree that someone would really listen and insist that he get help. Sometimes you never get a second chance to really listen to someone who is suffering deeply. I would have gone to his house and picked him up for coffee at 2 a.m. if that was what was needed. Clearly none of us were clued in enough.

Sometimes churches can hinder rather than help people. Often they desire to have their congregation conform to the precepts of the denomination first and do not hear what is going on with some of the members. For some people this conformity can place them in a position that is not best for their lives. If a couple really hates each other should they continue to be married at risk of suicide? I wonder. If getting a divorce would save your life should you not get one because it is contrary to the precepts of your church? I know that such thinking is highly controversial because I am saying that the people in authority sometimes do not have the best answers for our lives. We have to find our own way in our lives to protect our lives.

When people make vows before God to remain married, "until death us do part", do they adhere to those vows even if it means that one of them is going to kill him or herself rather than continue in the relationship? This is a very difficult question and one that millions of couples answer with divorce. If people get a second chance at life isn't divorce therefore an important option? What would God have you do? Certainly protecting your life is paramount. If you are depressed out of your mind in your marriage, would God want you to stay in that marriage? I think not but there are plenty of people that would never consider divorce regardless of the harm it might do to their soul or their very life. This is a very personal decision that must be weighed carefully within your chosen parameters.

I am not against churches and the teachings of Christ for our lives. I do believe however that sometimes churches can want things for people that do not validate the parishioners' lives and who they really are. I do not believe churches can or should try to change gay people into heterosexual people. I think God loves them just the way they are.

I have heard that some gay people contemplate suicide because they know they will never fit in their church exactly as they are. To me, this is completely contrary to the teachings of Jesus because Jesus was all inclusive, "That none should perish". That churches turn gay people away is morally unconscionable to me.

If your church or organization is not hearing what is really going on with you, perhaps it is best to find new friends, a new church or an organization that will welcome you exactly as you are. You cannot change other people you can only change yourself from the inside out. However if you in your life are not being validated in your life and your choices then you have to find where you will be validated.

Validation is a kind of affirmation of you exactly as you are. You do not have to change to please others; you do not have to be anyone that you aren't. You, as a child of the most high God, are worthy of validation exactly as you are with all of your faults, foibles, mistakes, history. Since all of us are similar in this regard, we all are deserving of this validation in our lives.

Listening ears can work wonders. What it does, I believe, is allow for changing your perspective even if only for a short time while you are with someone who is listening to you. It may not go to the root of the problem necessarily but what it does do is allow you to reformulate the problem in your head. Another person's perspective can shed some new light on what is going on in your life, so you can begin to get well again, through getting the help you need.

But, if you are helping by listening to someone with the idea that you can change the core of a person, who they really are, then I think you are sorely mistaken. The person hearing you will close you out quickly and sharply. You may frighten them for a while but they will come back stronger against you.

People who study communication know that deep listening is essential to communication among people. It is not just bouncing ideas off each other though that is part of it, it is going beneath the surface to something that is deeper and richer and more deeply edifying for both people. But it is also one human being nurturing another through words to help that person become exactly who they were meant to be.

A few days ago I was at a meeting where a person said that thoughts of suicide had popped up in his mind. He is a farmer and we have been in a terrible drought. The crops have been ruined and the only hope is to get money from the government so they do not go under. In the same period of time his favorite dog died. So he was facing two situations that were debilitating for him, loss of income and livelihood and grief over a pet. No wonder he was very down.

For me, the word suicide sent up a red flag. This person was telling us that he is in a dangerous state of mind and he needed attention soon. I called him soon thereafter, and just told him that I heard what he said and offered to pick him up any time of the day or night, go for coffee so he could talk as much as he needs to, until he runs out of words.

I think that preventing suicide is as easy as this, being alert and open to what people are really saying and making it clear to them that you care about them and will be there for them if they need to talk. There is no way to predict what they will ultimately do but we have to make the effort to help them when it is clear what is going on in their heads.

For me, as a Christian, I believe the Holy Spirit moves us to reach out to people when they are in need. It does not have to be a lot of attention but a little will go a long way. I am moved to take action and sometimes that action is only prayer for them but sometimes it is a call or a cup of coffee. Doing something is better than doing nothing.

Questions to journalize:

Do you know what deep listening is? Do you have this talent to share with others?

_____
_____
_____
_____
_____

Do you have someone in your life that you feel really listens to what is going on with you? Do you share this gift with someone close to you?

_____
_____
_____
_____
_____

Does your church or spiritual group accept you and others exactly as you are? Is there some way that you can teach them to do so?

_____
_____
_____
_____
_____

# Chapter 4

## The Descent Into Hell

What happens when a person decides to take their own life? I think a "Descent into Hell" is the closest thing I can think of that describes it.

What is the person obsessing about in their life? For me it was relationships. I became obsessive about the people I loved who I thought, mistakenly, loved me. After all, they were the center of my universe; certainly the same was true for them.

Both of my suicide attempts were after being rejected by the center of my obsession, two people I fell in love with at first sight. We quickly became friends in both cases. I imagined I would spend the rest of my life loving them and being extremely close friends, if not lovers, with them.

The rejection episodes were horrible events in my life that undercut the core of my being. I was given some piece of truth about this person that conflicted with what I knew and felt and didn't we have such a wonderful history together? I saw them as my reason for being, serving them in any way that I could whether it was small gifts, large gifts or something from my self that was irreplaceable. I saw them needing me to complete their lives; that I would be a resource for them that they would always need throughout eternity. I did not just want to be with them always but more to be them, shape them into images I could always give my life's mission to, integral to who I was going to be for the rest of my life.

I learned while studying religions that many people make other people their object of worship which according to the Judeo-Christian tradition is a serious sin against God, so serious it is one of the "Ten Commandments": "Thou shalt have no other gods before me." Practicing Buddhism taught me the same thing; you have to work on your own life from inside out. Nothing else will work.

In either religion and I believe this is true of virtually all religions, once we place our faith, our praise in something other than the Source of the Higher Power, then we lose our core being. It is as if we hand this core of our nature over to something or someone and we lose the very focus of our lives. Once we lose this focus of our lives in many ways we have already lost the core of our being and it is a short trip to the idea that when all goes wrong, to end the offending life condition, we can do so by ending our lives.

It took me years to get the focus of my life back on me. This is not a bad thing to have the focus of your life on yourself, it is essential. I think it goes to the depth of our primordial urges such as self protection, fight or flight instincts.

It is important to distinguish this focus of your life on you and selfishness. When the focus of your life is on you, you can begin to give to others in your life, you can begin to live because you are focused on your mission in your life. Selfishness, on the other hand, is focusing on getting your way, having instant gratification, always being the center of attention, and grabbing for things without concern for others. Understanding your motives in all things is taking an assessment of your life. As a life supporting activity assessing one's life is a life supporting activity that is the beginning of living an "examined life", an essential act for growth as a human being.

When the focus of my life has been on other people I have had physiological effects such as a terrible pit in my stomach that would never go away. I learned through counseling that to the degree that I put the focus of my life back on me the pit in my stomach would disappear. Over years it did disappear. When it rears its head I have only to look at my life and question my motives, my focus and ask tough questions. Who am I trying to please? For me when I am trying to please everyone around me but me, then the focus of my life is no longer on me.

When I was a young woman a couple I babysat for from my church was having a rough time in their lives at the time. I did not understand this concept, that "having a bad time in one's life" was just a period of time that would pass. It has always stuck with me that "having a bad time" is temporary; all you have to do is live through it. Pastor Joel Osteen says, "It did not come to stay, it came to pass."

When a person kills themselves I think their perception of this "having a bad time" is that it is going to go on forever and they can't stand the thought of it. I think it is a time for most people when they are most open to learning how to change their lives for the better, if they can only be distracted from the day to day misery of it. I have heard it said that a person goes through one of these periods of time every seven years the same way that our cells turn over every seven years. This can be seen as a time of renewing one's self, getting in touch with that core of one's being, deciding who you really want to be and what you want to do.

At this point I would like to say something about our military personnel whose lives are in danger everyday. Clearly they face death daily and often they are in physically dangerous places. I can see that they would want to give up and die; that they feel abandoned by our nation, and they are living in times that are not just bad but seemingly endless. Add to this they may not get the support they need from home. When they leave on their mission perhaps that alone is their "descent into hell" and perhaps they feel hopeless about it. Inevitably the situation is temporary though they may not believe it at the time. The ones that kill themselves must be in a particular kind of hell where they envision only the worst every day.

A prayer for them here and now: "Lord please protect the people in our military forces. When they feel hopeless, please put people in their paths to give them a new perspective. Please protect them from themselves and give them hope for their futures. Lord, may we as a nation give them the resources they need to protect their own lives by way of having support networks to help them every day. As a nation guide us to support them in the best ways possible, be supportive and communicative with them to the very best of our ability.

Questions to Journalize:

Write about your descent into Hell? Where are you in your life today?

_____

_____

_____

_____

_____


Do you know of a person in the military who would love to hear from you? What can you do to lighten their load? A note of caring can go a long way for them, to hear from home.

_____

_____

_____

_____

_____

# Chapter 5

## Reading The Signs

When someone is immersed in suicidal ideation and are planning their suicide they frequently give clues to what is going on inside themselves. It is during this time period that this person needs medical and psychological care. This is so important that, as I have mentioned elsewhere, it is worth the embarrassment or chastisement from the person to proceed with getting them help, even if it means hospitalization or commitment. At this point you are saving their life so it is a no-holds barred situation. Do what you must but do something.

While clues from this person may be as unique as they are, it is typical for someone who is contemplating suicide to do one or more of the following:

1. Depression is a clue. If you are severely depressed or your loved one is seriously depressed, get help! Depression is an indication that something is not right in the life of the suicidal person.
2. Pack up their things as if they are going on a trip.
3. Give away special things to people they want to have their favorite things.
4. Sell things that no one would imagine them selling. Treasured things.
5. Seek out people they care about or who care about them, present and past lovers, spouses, friends and family and say good-bye to them. They may be awkward about this but the person they are visiting may not have seen them in a long time and be very

surprised they have shown up. Later, they will understand that it was a good-bye visit and it might be quite meaningful to the loved one and the recipient.

6. In lieu of a visit they may write or email loved ones.

7. Do things that are out of character, unexpected, or unusual for them. Ordinarily such an action might be totally out of their realm and may be an indication of how deeply depressed they are. There is no way to guess what it might be and by nature it is something completely out of character for the person.

8. Refuse to do favorite activities with others, such as fishing or other common activities.

9. They may say things like, "Everyone would be better off without me." "What would you think if I just left town for good?" Again, there is no way to predict what they may say but the meaning will be clear that they are not planning on staying around for long.

10. Some people finish up with business commitments such as seeing their banker to close out their accounts, take out an additional insurance policy to provide for their kids, or other business type meetings.

11. People have been known to set out the clothes that they want to be buried in.

12. They may prepare a note to leave behind. This note could be written just before or they could take some time to prepare it, making certain they are saying exactly what they want to say.

13. They may stop taking medications they need to take, whether anti-depressants or medications they take for serious conditions.

14. They may contact a spiritual leader, pastor, priest or rabbi or other person they have relied on in their faith. This visit, too, may be a "good-bye" visit.

15. There may be something entirely unique they do that later will be understood as their way of preparing for leaving.

16. If your loved one is overseas, listen to them carefully when you are able to talk. What clues are they giving you that they are deeply depressed? Insist that they get help. The military has got to be opening their eyes to personnel that are "at risk".

It is essential to understand that this suicidal person may be absolutely private about the plans he or she is making. They may take a measure of pleasure in their plans but only as long as they remain private. In dealing with this person and getting them help, I think it is important to ask blatant questions such as: "Are you ok?" "Are you thinking of harming yourself?" "Do I need to call in help for you?" You may know what is best to use with your loved one, whatever it is now is the time to pull out all of the stops.

I suggest you have an action plan in place, preferably not shared with the person considering suicide, though a friend was once very clear with me, in my life, saying, "If I feel you have given me sufficient insight into the possibility that you may kill yourself, I will get help for you whether you like it or not, including hospitalization." You may need help getting your loved one to the hospital and the best thing to do is just call 911. They have a lot of experience that can help you get the person taken care of quickly. If you take the person to the hospital yourself, you run the risk of them harming you or jumping out of the car or taking other dangerous actions. Time is of the essence.

The loved one may have been planning suicide for a long time or it could be a spontaneous or immediate response to something in their life that is not right. Regardless, getting them help quickly is paramount.

I have heard people say that the people that talk about suicide never attempt it but the people who keep their plans completely private are more likely to attempt it. I think anyone who threatens it or someone who is seemingly planning it in a private way have to be taken absolutely seriously. A red flag is a red flag is a red flag.

Also I believe the statistic is that people who have attempted suicide in the past are at greater risk for attempting it again. A person that thinks about suicide frequently is at greater risk because the thoughts are taking up space in their mind, at the forefront of their thoughts. They may feel they failed before but they will not fail next time. A little awareness can go a long way in helping this person.

There is no way to know exactly what is going on in the mind of someone in danger of killing themselves. We can not see into someone else's brain, no matter how close we are, especially if they are doing their best to hide what is going on. While we cannot second guess them, nor do we want to live in a state of heightened panic about them, we simply have to do our best on their behalf. No more and no less is required.

Remember there is no shame in erring on the side of caution. If the person is successful at killing him or herself you would ask if there was something you could have done. Would you have done it? If you could have done something and didn't, wouldn't you then have terrible guilt for a long time? If you are in a place to be of help, then help.

Sometimes a person that we don't particularly know or like will give us information we would rather not have. Do we just walk away? I think not. If God has placed this person in our path are we not to consider how we can help them? I think God has his angels working with us everyday in every way to be of use to Him. What would we say to God when we meet Him? "I was too busy?" "I didn't know him or like him?"

When I finally get to heaven I want to hear God say, "Well done thou good and faithful servant." I hope you do too.

Questions to Journalize:

Have you heard your loved one say something that is a clue to what is going on inside them related to suicidal ideation?

_____

_____

_____

_____

_____

If you hear such words, do you have an action plan in place? Talk to his or her doctor in advance of ever needing them. What action steps would you take? If you need help to initiate such steps who will you call to help you?

_____

_____

_____

_____

_____

# Chapter 6

# The Moments Just Before

Both times I attempted suicide I remember crying and screaming so much that I had the distinct feeling that I was out of my mind. I was in a place in my brain where the act of suicide took over my brain and I was determined to proceed. I think it is at this crucial moment that you have to divert yourself or your loved one.

Of course there are a million ways to divert yourself or someone else, the point is simply to do it. If you do something simple like deep breathing then you can stop crying and divert your mind.

This state of being out of one's mind is the most dangerous place in the world. I think it is the place where everyone who has attempted suicide and either succeeded or not succeeded has known. It is the deepest darkest pit of the mind that must be moved away from.

If you are in this state, get help immediately. Call 911, the police, a local hospital, just get help. There is a point of "no return" where demons take over your mind and push you toward killing yourself. Do something to keep you from getting to that point.

Questions to Journalize:

Have you personally been in this space before? What did you do to get yourself out of it?

_____

_____

_____

_____

_____

Would you recognize this space if you saw someone else in it? What would you do if you saw them in a very distressed and depressed state? How would you protect them? How would you protect them from themselves?

_____

_____

_____

_____

_____

# Chapter 7

## Yer Kids

If you end your life and you have children, those children will grow up or mature into human beings with a hole in their hearts where you used to live. It is unavoidable. If they remember anything at all about you, this will be the thing they remember most. And they will remember all of the details.

Children love their parents unconditionally from birth. If you choose to reject them and the rest of the people in your life they have no choice but to remember you at your last time together.

I have heard that suicide is the most selfish thing you can do. It is centered on you not getting your needs met in your life somehow and punishing everyone in your life by taking you out of the picture. If you remove yourself, there are no options for decision making, figuring things out together, endless talking, compromising, learning. You rob them and their future from all of the possibilities that life could have offered with you. Don't do it.

While your children may forgive you after time has passed and they may rationalize that you were very sick, even out of your mind, they will not forget what you did to them. And you are doing it to them too. Taking you out of the picture harms them for the rest of their lives and beyond. They will be explaining your absence to their friends and loved ones for the rest of their lives. Your children's children will not have a grandfather or grandmother and they will resent that as they grow older too.

If you are thinking about suicide, get help now. When you are in the realm of thinking about suicide, giving the idea credibility, you push yourself forward in that direction. Stop your thinking about it immediately and get help.

Rage. At some point your family may become enraged at you. You deprived them of the opportunity to help you with whatever was going on with you. Your parents, spouse, or even former spouses and of course your children or grandchildren want to help you through whatever it is you are going through. Give them an opportunity to help you. Life is worth it. When you are immersed in suicidal ideation you cannot see a way out and may rationalize that everything would be better without you. This is a fallacy, get help to get out of it.

Questions to Journalize:

Do you really know how much your kids love you and would miss you? Do you understand that you will break their hearts for the rest of their lives?

_____

_____

_____

_____

_____

Do you understand they will blame themselves and ask forever what they could have done to stop you?

_____

_____

_____

_____

_____

Do you understand that they would do anything on earth to help you?

_____

_____

_____

_____

_____

Can you ask them for their attention? Can you make a list of what you need from them? Can you begin to ask for what you need from them? While this can seem like an impossible task, you could break it down into very small parts. "I need to have you help me take the dog for a walk." I need to tell you a story about my life." Kids can be a rapt audience and will divert what is going on with them to meet your needs. Ask them!

_____

_____

_____

_____

_____

# Chapter 8

# "It Is Only Money, Honey."

My mother, who grew up during the First Great Depression lived in farm shacks on acreages, is fond of saying, when things are most down financially, "It is only money, Honey." This from a woman that had only one dress for school and 2 pairs of underwear and two pairs of socks; one was in the process of drying while the other one was worn to school. When she got divorced from my dad in the 1970's and was on her own for years she struggled a lot to feed, clothe, and house my siblings. In some ways she got really creative about money and in some ways she got really tight fisted with it; full of common sense about what you could and could not have on a secretary's salary. I am so proud of her for living through this tough time and showing her children how to do the same.

In my 23 years as a Realtor® I have seen the market fluctuate wildly, I have seen really good times and really bad times. For those of us in sales professions it has been a time of feast or famine, mostly famine or what we joke about in my office as: "Chicken today, feathers tomorrow." To say it has been difficult is a huge understatement; bills continue to mount whether or not people are buying houses.

During these years I have known of two people who have killed themselves over failure in the market place, the market going south and tough times surrounding them. There may have been many more but these two were the only ones that I knew of where it was not a secret about what happened to them.

Was there anything we could have done about it to prevent these people from taking their lives? I don't know. They were both deeply depressed and in situations that were seemingly hopeless. By my own history I would have liked to talk with them and point them in the direction of good mental health, getting help and figuring out with them what they needed to do for themselves.

Sometimes we are seemingly with our backs up against the wall having the pulp beaten out of us. I think every person that has gone through foreclosure on a house is or was at this crossroad where they may have considered ending the shame, harassment and the awful feelings. I do not think they would be normal human beings if they had not felt hopeless and humiliated.

Fortunately there are forces in our nation that are trying to lessen the numbers of people in this horrible situation. Godspeed for the resolution of their problems.

Business failure is common these days and there is a 70% failure rate for Realtors within the first 3 years. And that after you have spent thousands on dues, advertising, marketing, the whole works. It is a pain to be reckoned with but not one to take your life over. If you are in such a mess, get help. Do something.

Money is amorphous and fleeting. Like the joke, "Money talks-mine says good-bye!" it is best to wear financial burden like a loose garment. "This too shall pass" and we never know when it will change. Be open to change in your life.

Questions to Journalize:

Are you in a financial mess that is seemingly hopeless? Do you sometimes think everything would be better if you were dead?

_____

_____

_____

_____

_____

What action steps can you take today that will lighten your weary load?

_____

_____

_____

_____

_____

# Chapter 9

# Mental Illness

I think that by definition that someone who wants to kill themselves or attempts suicide is by nature mentally ill. If you want to destroy your life then you are by nature off your center, losing site of the core of your self, and therefore need serious help. If the focus of your life is on another person, alcohol, drugs or another addictive source then the focus of your life is no longer on you, your dreams and your future.

When someone is mentally ill they need help. It is not shameful to get help however you can so that you can become well again. Checking into or being admitted into a psychiatric ward in your community may be the very thing that puts you on a path to your wellness again. You can view such hospitalization as being imprisoned or you can view it as time out in which you are going to learn how to protect your life from you. Perspective is always important.

When a person has been diagnosed with a mental illness they can begin to help themselves get well again. Today's pharmacopoeia has a plethora of medical solutions that will help with symptoms. If you need to be on medication for depression, take it, grow into how it can help you. Seeing a counselor while taking a medication can have double the benefit for getting well again.

Questions to journalize:

Have you been deeply depressed, especially for a long time? Do you or does someone dear to you have a mental illness? What action steps can you, and do you want to take?

_____

_____

_____

_____

_____

# Chapter 10

# Depression And Suicide

While Depression is considered to be a mental illness, many people live in depression all the time and would never be considered mentally ill because they might be considered to be "high functioning".

Many people do get help for depression, recognizing they are not on "top of their game". Typically they visit a psychologist or psychiatrist for a period of time, work out some of the problems that have them depressed, go on an anti-depressant which more or less helps them.

But I think they are most at risk for suicide. If they have been depressed and unhappy for long periods of time they may begin to believe it will never change and suicide looks appealing to end it all. Suicidal ideation may have already crept into their thinking and they may dwell on it for long periods of time, though not telling anyone or disclosing what is really going on.

This sense of privacy cannot be overlooked. There are people who will not disclose what is going on with them because they live in a world of shame and humiliation. There are people that will not admit that things are terribly wrong with their lives even though everything may appear fine. If a person is deeply depressed and they are not getting help for it, their sense of privacy may be invaded if they are pushed. Treat them with the greatest amount of respect that you can, but begin to ask questions, some can even be lighthearted so they laugh or smile, "Are you in some kind of funk?" "What can I do to help you out of it?" As a friend you may know of something that will please them and be able to move them toward getting help.

I personally believe you can look a person in the eyes and see if they are depressed. Their eyes may appear downcast, slightly closed and somewhat drowsy. Because our eyelids act with involuntary muscle movements, I think it is impossible to hide what is really going on inside, from the eyes to the brain. Looking down seems to be a clue to what is going on inside. While it is metaphorical, this "looking down" is also physiological.

Depression is a very treatable malady today with many options available. At the base of it though is the question about how honest you are being with yourself and others about what is going on with you. You have to admit that you are depressed in order to begin to seek help for it. You may live in a community, family, work environment that does not take depression seriously. If so, trust your gut and get help anyway.

Questions to Journalize:

Do you recognize when you are depressed or down? What do you do to get yourself out of it?

_____

_____

_____

_____

_____

Would you get help if you felt you needed it? What are some action steps you would take?

_____

_____

_____

_____

_____

# Chapter 11

# Drugs And Alcohol

I think one of the reasons that the 12 step programs are so effective is that the alcohol or drug abuser can readily see that there-in lies an opportunity to start over in their lives. "The Land of Beginning Again," is a state of mind when you are at the bottom of your pit, you can begin to believe that you can dig yourself out again.

Many people who do drugs or alcohol for an extended period of time know that they are walking a fine line between life and death. Too much alcohol can kill you quickly or slowly in much the same way a drug overdose can kill you immediately.

Suicide from alcohol and drugs are legendary from Marilyn Monroe to Jim Morrison or Curt Cobain. There is a point where the substance takes over and creates a situation where the abuser is at death's door, ready to give in to the substance, give up and die. I think there is a point of no-return where if immediate help is not obtained they will die. The combination of drugs and alcohol will go to the heart and stop it. Clearly a person that wants deeply enough to die may very well succeed because they may fall asleep or pass out before they can ask for help or before someone finds them.

Stopping them may be virtually impossible unless they have someone watching them closely. Yet even this is would be nearly impossible to ensure. The recent death of Amy Winehouse is an example of someone who had people around her watching her nearly all the time and yet she still succeeded in killing herself.

When a person is out of their mind, in the deepest pit, and incapable at that time of getting themselves out, the possibility of someone intervening diminishes. Which is why it is so important that if your loved one is "at risk", they not be left alone, be hospitalized if necessary or placed in a treatment center.

Since alcoholics and drug abusers can refuse treatment and walk away from facilities, sometimes they have to be court-ordered to accept treatment. This is a relatively simple procedure where you go to your county courthouse, meet with the staff, fill out papers and then the police will escort them to a hospital or treatment center. At least at the hospital they will be seen rather quickly by medical personnel where it will be determined if they need to be restrained to prevent them from harming themselves. A few days later there will be a hearing with a court appointed judge who will determine. when and whether they should be released and under what conditions.

Some time ago people would be released with the condition they begin attending a 12 step program such as AA, Narc-Anon or Al-Anon. The 12 Step programs are based on taking one day at a time, staying out of the first drink or first hit, sharing the experience strength and hope of members between those attending. This paradigm has worked for millions of people and can be a major step toward getting well again, beginning again. The substance abuser has to do their part too and that is being honest, open and willing to get help. Sometimes people do go right back out only to try to abuse again, or experiment with trying to find a different solution. Some people have to go back to square one many times until something sinks in for them and they take the help that is offered. Anyone addicted to alcohol or drugs knows that it is an easy walk to kill themselves if they do not get help. They have to want to live out their lives and sometimes this takes a while for them to grasp. There are people who struggle with this for a long time. And there are people that ultimately do kill themselves. However if they get into a good group the likelihood of that happening diminishes over time. Living "One Day at a Time" staying out of the First Drink or Hit, can save lives and it has.

When I was younger I was under the delusion that getting drunk would lessen the pain I was feeling at the time over whatever had befallen me. Somehow I thought that crying while drunk was cathartic, removing the pain from my life situations. I think it is a delusion that a lot of people share.

But it was an absolute fallacy. Nothing ever got better or changed in significant ways from getting drunk. All that happened was that I would get a terrible headache and hangover and still have to face the problems in the new day, but now with increased embarrassment over bad behavior.

So I learned in AA to face the problems head on, deal with my life as honestly as I could and life would improve over time, and it did. Life is not a bowl of cherries at times but at least it is not falling down drunk, miserable and crying.

Many times people do not recognize that they are alcoholics or drug abusers until they get jailed and fined for drunk driving. As painful and expensive as this experience is, it can be a real catalyst for the substance abuser to take inventory, buck up and get help. In the long run it can be a major blessing but that is a different perspective entirely.

Alcohol is a depressant and as such it will cause a person to go into a pit of depression if used long enough and hard enough. It cannot be overcome instantly as it takes time to be relieved of the craving and obsession. But with daily work on this, alcoholics and drug abusers can and do get well.

Questions to Journalize:

Do you try to live your life, one day at a time? What skills help you to do so?

_____

_____

_____

_____

_____

Do you turn to drugs and alcohol to help you get through tough times? What other coping skills do you have at your disposal?

_____

_____

_____

_____

_____

# Chapter 12

# Bullying

Whenever teenagers decide life is not worth living and kill themselves I become infuriated. Who, at school, was not watching what was going on? How can bullying go on beneath their noses and they do not notice? Teachers have to pay attention to students who are at risk. Who is being picked on incessantly? Who is withdrawn, different for whatever reason, and why is harassment allowed to continue? It has to stop. School is a bad enough experience for many youth without daily being harassed and harangued. Can we ask teachers to be more aware of what is going on? Absolutely yes! They are charged with teaching the children, how can they not also be charged with figuring out what is going on in school? These are smart people for the most part.

In recent years there have been an increasing number of young people that commit suicide after being bullied. Schools are becoming more aware and creating policies and programs to protect young people in school but one death is too many. Parents listen to your kids! They will give you clues to how they are being treated in school or after school. Get used to talking to them about what is happening in their days and be prepared to do something to protect your child.

When I was in junior high school I had several boys that would harass me after school because of the birth defect I had. They had their own ugly names they called me. To this day I understand when a young person shoots their harasser. There was a time when I would have shot my harassers if I had had any idea on how to obtain and use a gun. Thank God that was not in the picture at the time. Eventually my mother listened to me about what was happening and talked with their mothers. Only then did it stop for good.

Questions to Journalize:

Do you know of someone who is presently being bullied? What resources are available to you to help stop it?

_____

_____

_____

_____

_____

Were you bullied as a youth? What did you do to stop it?

_____

_____

_____

_____

_____

# Chapter 13

# Cutting

In recent years I personally have known of young people, especially young women who have been addicted to cutting themselves.

I think that when a person cuts their wrists, arms or other parts other body they are really attempting suicide in miniature. They are attempting to negate themselves by inflicting extreme pain on themselves short of killing themselves successfully.

I have heard this activity rationalized as creating pain that is greater than the emotional pain they are presently experiencing, thereby keeping their pain in perspective, or prioritized. "This pain is worse than that pain" is one of the excuses I have heard.

There are ways they attempt to disguise their self mutilation with large bandages, bandages made from colorful scarves, long sleeves and other materials to hide the cutting and scarring. A person that has her forearms, wrists and arms covered up all the time may be covering up cutting and attention should be paid to her to protect her from herself.

It is a cry out for attention and help and should always be taken seriously by friends and loved ones. It is important to be tuned into what is going on with the person that is cutting. What else are they doing that is outside the norm?

Questions to Journalize:

Do you or does your loved one participate in cutting behaviors?

------------------------------------------------
------------------------------------------------
------------------------------------------------
------------------------------------------------
------------------------------------------------

What are your reasons or theirs? Who can you go to for help on this?

------------------------------------------------
------------------------------------------------
------------------------------------------------
------------------------------------------------
------------------------------------------------

# Chapter 14

## A Special Note For Seniors

One of the delights of my life was being the Activities Coordinator for a senior program in Oberlin, Ohio for many years. My function was to provide activities for seniors that would help them stay active and healthy for as long as possible. We focused on activities that were somewhat challenging, intriguing and fun and that allowed seniors to reattach to life from wherever they were. Many had lost spouses, family members, friends, loved ones, of course income and jobs, position, health, and unfortunately a lot of validation in life. This is all a part of life but it is also a very most painful part.

While we all must face the end of our lives the most important thing, in my opinion is to face it joyfully, with or without loved ones, ready for whatever the universe has unfolding for us. I love the little joke about coming into death turning the corner on two tires, used up and ready to go, no regrets.

Seniors are especially at risk for suicidal ideation because many are isolated, sometimes do not see enough people in their daily lives, or do not have enough going on. As a society seniors are often overlooked except when we need something from them, i.e. their numbers as a voting block, or their proactive fighters on certain issues under the umbrella of AARP.

Often times the fact that they are "at risk" for suicide is generally overlooked in the whole of our communities. It basically goes unnoticed because of their age and level of frailty. An extra pill here or there, too many sleeping medications, or other potential life ending substances are available. Self-medicating may be a way of trying to harness some of the control they have lost over their lives, especially in their bodies and minds.

Another problem with seniors is them not getting the medical care they know they need. I knew a woman with a heart condition who had had small heart attacks but she did not get medical care for them. The last heart attack killed her. Was this a form of suicide? I don't know, only that she was highly intelligent and I believe knew what was going on with her heart. She was ready to die at her age but did she go earlier by choice?

Seniors are every bit as subject to deep and serious depression as any other age group. Seniors need treatment as much as any other age group so they can live out their days on an even keel despite all that has happened or is happening to them.

Senior programs need to be on the alert for people that are suffering deeply with treatable problems to ensure the senior's life is protected from themselves if necessary. Senior care programs can put you in contact with gerontology specialists in your area if you need them. These specialists are trained to look deeper at the concerns of aging people. As a nation we need to take the issues of seniors seriously.

Little things can be life-savers for seniors: having people check up on them on occasion if not on a daily basis, regular routines, places where they will be expected to be. Home visitors. Making sure they are getting the health care they need, by asking them.

Having activities to attend is very important for many seniors. They can visit with their peers, have some fun doing something together and maintain their mental and physical health doing so.

My 93 year old grandmother used to go to her church regularly for some senior activities. They got together and played games they liked, had coffee and a treat of some kind and made certain they got to and from their homes ok afterwards. She loved meeting with these women and men. She loved it so much that she would talk to various ones in the evening when she was home alone. Her caring for her peers and their caring for her was an immense blessing to her and I am certain gave her her good outlook on life and her longevity.

Questions to journalize:

Do you know or are you a senior that may be at risk for ending your life?

---------------------------------------------------------------
---------------------------------------------------------------
---------------------------------------------------------------
---------------------------------------------------------------
---------------------------------------------------------------

What are some action steps you can take?

---------------------------------------------------------------
---------------------------------------------------------------
---------------------------------------------------------------
---------------------------------------------------------------
---------------------------------------------------------------

Do you meet on a regular basis with your friends or peer group? If not, is there some activity you would like to start?

---------------------------------------------------------------
---------------------------------------------------------------
---------------------------------------------------------------
---------------------------------------------------------------
---------------------------------------------------------------

Churches are excellent places to set up some group activities. My church for instance has a well attended group "Tuesday Coffee and Conversation" Group that is beloved by the attendees. It is an opportunity for members to check in with each other, participate in a group discussion, but on a much deeper level simply to care about each other in their day to day lives. This is just an example, what would you like to see in your community?

---------------------------------------------------------------
---------------------------------------------------------------
---------------------------------------------------------------
---------------------------------------------------------------
---------------------------------------------------------------

# Chapter 15

# A Special Note For Veterans

Just recently I heard on the news that the number of suicides of military personnel have surpassed the numbers of war combat deaths. This is shocking to me. It makes me feel that these people are facing a special hell in our military that they feel will never get better so that killing themselves, having control over their deaths is easier than facing the potential death in a war.

If you are a service person your tour of duty will end eventually. If you are in danger of suicide during your tour, get help. Contact medical personnel or a chaplain. Tell someone at home as that person could possibly do something to help stateside.

When you serve our country we as a nation owe you a debt of respect that we can pay back in certain ways. Getting you help when you need it is one of them. Push for the help you need because we want you to have it. Our military budget is so large that certainly the mental health of our troops must be a top priority.

Questions to Journalize:

How can you take good care of yourself especially your mental health, while in the military?

_____

_____

_____

_____

_____

Who can you contact for help if you are in danger? What are your resources? Can you identify several helping resources that you can take advantage of?

_____

_____

_____

_____

_____

Are you having nightmares or other things happening in your mind or sleep that you know are not right for you?

_____

_____

_____

_____

_____

# Chapter 16

# Medical Suicide

When a person has suffered more than any human being should ever have to, such as with cancer, the question comes up about whether they should be allowed or in some way encouraged to take their own life. I say no for a lot of reasons.

Having been a hospice volunteer I have seen where dying patients can have a reprieve of sorts from their illness in the last days or hours. It can be a time where they connect with family and loved ones for the last time and the experience for all can be really loving, kind, forgiving, full and rewarding. Why deny the dying person this last special time?

I do believe however, that people should have living wills so that medical personnel are aware of the patient's last wishes to not be resuscitated or kept unnecessarily alive. All of this is a matter of personal choice and decision-making between the dying person and his or her family, loved ones and the doctor or caregivers. But the discussion needs to take place long before you need to rely on the decisions made.

My point is that I do not believe a person should take his or her own life for any reason. There may yet be life experiences to unfold that may be cherished for years to come. This is an extremely complex issue and I am not doing it justice here; if this is an important issue for you, please read up on it. Many good resources are available.

Many people are of a faith and religious background that strongly forbids suicide regardless of the circumstances. I understand that in Catholicism there is a redemptive quality about living out your life to its natural end no matter how bad it becomes. God is the ultimate source for the end of life questions, so therefore it is His will when He will take us to him. Though not Catholic, I agree with this.

Palliative care is about taking care of people at the end of life where comfort is the main concern; pain is reduced through self monitoring medication systems, for administering the most powerful of pain killers such as morphine. There is no reason for the dying person to experience excruciating pain when death is eminent or projected for the near future.

Hospice care has come out of its historical closet and is now an option for most people. Hospice care is sort of the way things have always been done since the beginning of time; when a person was near death, family and friends would care for them at home, making them as comfortable as possible The act of caring for a person at home allowed everyone in the dying person's environment to take a more active role in caregiving since the dying person was likely nearby. Last days and hours were family times of communicating among themselves. I think Hospice brings back a level of awe in the death and dying process; no more do people have to be separated from loved ones at inconvenient times. There is a sense of belonging on the part of all participants that cannot be duplicated in nursing homes. Death is not so much a medical event to be controlled and manipulated but just a part of life as natural as life itself.

You must speak up about what your wants and needs are in this case; as much as Hospice workers try to foresee your wants and needs this is not always possible and sometimes they need reminders or greater understanding.

When my grandmother of 94 passed away she spent about the last four days of her life in a beautiful hospice care center in my community. During these days people from all over the country came to visit and be with her and the rest of our family. At times we had over 30 people there in the room, the visiting area and the kids' area. (Try having 30 people over for an intimate discussion in a hospital room.)We all got as much time with her as we wanted. She was given morphine on a regular basis to ease her pain. I held her hand when she passed and just being there for her has meant everything to me. Don't rob your family and friends of the opportunity to serve you in your final hours. It will mean so much to them.

Questions to Journalize:

Do you have a "Living Will"- What would it take for you to put one together?

_____

_____

_____

_____

_____

Have you thought about what you want your end of life care to be?

_____

_____

_____

_____

_____

# Part 2
# Getting The Help You Need

# Chapter 17

# The Vow

On my second suicide attempt I swallowed a lot of pills, was rushed to the hospital where I was given Ipecac and threw them up.

When I returned home several friends were waiting there for me. One dear friend, an older woman, made me make a vow with her that if I ever got this bad again I would seek professional help. She and others there insisted that I start counseling with an excellent counselor which I did the next day.

I saw this psychologist for nearly two years and she helped me change my life. She identified that I had my life focused on the object of my love to the degree that I had a terrible empty feeling in my stomach and soul. I was so sick in this relationship that I had lost myself in it and hence my reason for living when it ended.

This act of handing over the source or our being to another person in a relationship is very common among women in particular. There is a point where we cease to exist except as an appendage to the MAN. Or WOMAN, in lesbian relationships.

There is a point where the relationship is obsessive and compulsive and all encompassing. There is no reason to live except for the relationship.

There is a point where a person has crossed a line into insanity, depravity, depression where life itself is worth little. At the point of attempting suicide, I believe, there is a loss of self that is so deep that only demons remain and they are the ones that force the person to kill herself. It is as if there is a loss of consciousness that is all encompassing and debilitating. It is as if you are falling into a pit where you cannot get out, you can only give up and die. This was my experience of this place in my head where I no longer want to go.

Questions to journalize:

Do you have someone in your life with whom you want to make this vow? Is there anything holding you back from doing so? What would it take for you to take this step with someone else?

_____
_____
_____
_____
_____

Do you want to make this vow for your own life with someone else? Do you know of someone you can trust with this vow?

_____
_____
_____
_____
_____

# Chapter 18

## Selecting A Psychologist Or Psychiatrist

I have been blessed with two psychologists in my life that saved my life under different circumstances. In each case they figured out what was wrong with me and moved me to get the focus of my life back on me. I had become so obsessed in the relationships I was in that when those relationships ended I felt my life had ended too and that all that was left to be done was for me to leave life behind.

How do you select a really good psychologist or psychiatrist? First off if you are blessed enough to have insurance that will cover mental health issues such as depression you may be able to see a psychiatrist depending on the parameters of your insurance company. Psychiatrists are the most expensive of mental health care providers and your insurance company may not cover this and require that you see a psychologist instead.

My first experience with a psychologist was at the insistence of women friends when I was in college, after my second suicide attempt. They knew of a woman that was really good with the kinds of problems I was having and they recommended her. Fortunately she was able to see me quickly and to set up regular appointments with me.

I think the best mental health care providers figure out how to get you back to being your true self, a non-depressed person focused on his or her goals and dreams and making efforts to see those goals and dreams come to fruition. Through the sessions they encourage you by listening to you deeply, discovering where your self-esteem took a tangent off the circle of life that is you and helping you get back on track. They may encourage you to journalize what is happening with you on a day to day basis. This process of journalizing has been shown to have huge benefits as you can check your progress over time or see where you need more help. Good stuff.

Years later I went to a second psychologist who I met through the county mental health program in my community. I was blessed again with a really insightful woman who reiterated what I had learned years before and added so much. Because I found her through the mental health care services locally, her fee was on a sliding scale. I could never have afforded to pay her what she might have received in her own practice. This time I did not have health insurance, so this sliding scale arrangement was extremely beneficial for me.

In both cases I had women psychologists that were very much tuned in to the needs of women. I was comfortable with them and was able to be honest enough with them to get some serious help.

For me, I felt that it was best that I be under the care of women psychologists, thinking they would understand me better than a male psychologist or psychiatrist.

In both cases I felt that I had made the best choices for me; what is best for you is up to you to decide. Some people may need to see male mental health care providers especially if they want to talk to someone who may assert a more authoritarian persona. This was not the case for me.

If things are not working out with the person you are meeting with, it is important to recognize it and find someone else. You are there to get well and you must find someone you can trust with the deepest secrets of your life. If you do not feel you can be absolutely honest in your discovery, find someone else. When your life is in danger you want the very best care to help you get well. This is too important a decision to take lightly in any way.

A really good psychologist can really save your life at the worst possible time in your life. It is your right to expect excellent care that will help you over the long run of your life. Don't settle for less.

There are Christian psychologists who align themselves with other Christian psychologists in group practices. If this appeals to you it is worth checking out. Their focus, I believe, is helping you within a Christian context, perhaps praying with you or reading applicable Bible texts to help you through your problems.

Though I am a Christian I have never been to a psychologist in one of these practices. I do not want to subject myself and my psyche to shame-based treatment; I can guilt trip myself well enough alone. I grew up in a lot of shame- based faith practices in an entirely dysfunctional family that I no longer need to have that in my life. But you must judge for yourself. My experience is my experience, you must decide for yourself what works best for you.

Questions to journalize:

Do you have a psychologist or psychiatrist in mind? Is there something holding you back from seeing him or her?

_____

_____

_____

_____

_____

If not a psychologist or psychiatrist, do you have someone in your life that you can talk through your problems with?

_____

_____

_____

_____

_____

# Chapter 19

# The Void

Whatever you choose to call it, there is a feeling that I know I got that was palpable, the pit in my stomach, the empty feeling, the lost feeling or THE VOID.

The Void is about feeling empty at rejection, loss of the object of our love, loss of the focus of our life. The Void can feel so awful that the only response to it is to negate it through suicide or so we think.

I think the Void is the loss of the Self. It is a place where we feel so empty that we feel we have nothing to live for anymore.

It is a terrible and terrifying space to be in. If you lose your self, how you define your SELF can be utter emptiness. If you look in a mirror you might not be there it is such a feeling of loss.

I am sure that when we go through grief, grief is also coming face to face with aloneness and the Void. When a spouse dies the remaining spouse may feel their reason for being is now gone and the Void sets in. Only by becoming reattached to life, getting the focus of your life back on you, can you begin to get well again.

Questions to Journalize:

How do you describe the void in you when you are experiencing it?

_____

_____

_____

_____

_____

What do you do in your life to lessen the feeling of The Void? What action steps can you take to diminish it?

_____

_____

_____

_____

_____

# Chapter 20

# Getting Help

Whatever it takes to get you better is what is necessary. Sometimes people need to check into a Psych Ward of a hospital in order to prevent themselves from harming themselves further.

In my community there is a Mental Health Agency where you can go and pay for visits on a sliding scale. I paid $2.00 a week for a Psychologist visit a week that outside of this agency would have cost me from $100. to $200 an hour. When you are broke, $2.00 can be a lot of money.

There is help at a very low cost. There are even groups in places that are free. We have suicide hotlines you can call or prayer lines where people will pray with you and all of this is free. There is a national suicide hotline which if you call it they will connect you to local services in your own community.

If you are alcoholic addicted to alcohol or drugs, or related to one, please try Alcoholics Anonymous or Al-Anon Family Groups. It is an excellent way for you to examine your life, get in touch with your spiritual self and begin to heal yourself with the help of other people in similar situations. These groups are extremely popular, available and helpful evidenced by the fact that they exist all over the world. A basic premise is that anonymity gives people the freedom to examine their lives in an absolutely honest way; they can speak freely about what is going on and be encouraged by others who have been in similar situations.

The 12 step programs are self-sustaining through member contributions. They pass the basket and most people give $1.00 but it is not required at all. They say if you have nothing to contribute, keep coming back and someday you will

Through one of the Crisis Centers in my community there is a depression group that meets weekly for free with a licensed therapist. It is an offshoot of the National Alliance for the Mentally Ill, or NAMI.

There is good help available at very low cost or no cost. With so many people not having insurance of any kind these days, these alternatives are excellent choices in order to have more options.

It is critical that anyone seeking help know that their information is held in strictest confidentiality and anonymity. Virtually everyone in the groups are dealing with varying degrees of depression, suicidal ideation and various life problems, divorce, grief, loss of jobs, health, legal problems, and other related issues. The feeling of like-kind of problems can be a release to the newcomer that they have finally found someone that can understand where they are coming from.

Last, there is nothing embarrassing or helpless or shaming about getting help. To not get help is the insane thing.

Questions to journalize:

Do you have some action steps you want to take in your life? Where would you like to begin?

-------------------------------------------------------------
-------------------------------------------------------------
-------------------------------------------------------------
-------------------------------------------------------------
-------------------------------------------------------------

In designing your own wellness journey, what appeals most to you with regard to getting help? You are on a mission to save your own life or the life of someone you love. What calls out to you?

-------------------------------------------------------------
-------------------------------------------------------------
-------------------------------------------------------------
-------------------------------------------------------------
-------------------------------------------------------------

# Chapter 21

# Church

Many people look to their church when life is toughest for them. Somehow they have been taught over time to develop coping skills such as prayer, reading the Bible, meeting with their priest or pastor for direction in terrible times, or with lay members or prayer warriors.

I have been in churches that place a strong emphasis on developing "prayer warriors" people who can and will pray with you in a time of crisis. I want to be a prayer warrior to help others in my life and sometimes I am.

If you have this background it may be easiest to plug yourself back into it in order to survive the time you are going through now. I have seen people who seem to get through life's toughest times using these coping skills.

But, I have also seen people that I thought had these skills only to learn of their suicide. Sometimes the person going through the hell of suicide and preparation for it is separated from the truth of what is really going on with themselves. They may be deluded about many issues in their lives. Prayer is supposed to be about getting really honest with yourself, seeking out the will of God for your life.

Wherever you are on the issue of church the most important thing is to find something in your life that works for you that you can go to to avoid suicide. If you do not have a good relationship with your church or have the coping skills they endeavor to teach, then do not go to them. You do not want to make things worse for yourself. Church is such a private choice that you should do only what you feel is best for you.

However, there may be a guardian angel among the prayer warriors and you would not want to miss having that person in your life.

Many people grow up in families where church was regularly scheduled as something you automatically did every Sunday and sometimes on other days as well. I think it is important for children to have a relationship with a church that will give them coping strategies when their lives are in trouble. The point of the coping strategies is to help them learn how to rely on God in their lives, not only when they need Him, but woven into the entire fabric of their lives. I think this is as it should be though this is not always the case.

Some people have a guilt ridden relationship with the idea of church and by extension with God. They fear the punishment of church hierarchy and of God. Some of this goes back to the foundations of their faith, whether God is a loving and forgiving God or whether he is waiting to punish you for all of your wrong doings.

How you deal with church is a very private issue but if it is not working for you, I want to reiterate that I think it is best to find a new church or a new religion. Faith is supposed to help people throughout their lives, not harm them. If you feel your church is harming you then find another church.

In recent years there has been plenty in the media about church leaders molesting children. No wonder people want nothing to do with some churches. While this behavior is insidious and reprehensible, other church relationships can be very damaging as well. Sometimes women in a church get too close to the Pastor. While these relationships may be cloaked in ardor for the church, something else can be happening. Women can fall in love with the Pastor to the point of having relationships with pastors and leaders that can destroy whole congregations. Women can have a transference of their deepest emotions From their marriage and their relationship to God onto their religious leader, their pastor.

Only a pastor who really understands human relationships can recognize what is going on and correct it. This is ugly stuff, but the shame and self condemnation can be so deep for these women that they consider suicide.

You have to figure out for yourself where you stand with the whole idea of church. What is your purpose there? Are the relationships in the church healthy and edifying or derogatory and diminishing of your soul? Always be asking yourself about what is best for you, especially if you have already been through the "valley of the shadow of death".

Questions to journalize:

Do you attend church? If you do what is your relationship with your church and its members?

_____

_____

_____

_____

_____

Do you have the freedom to address issues that concern you at your church? Is it time for you to find a new church?

_____

_____

_____

_____

_____

# Chapter 22

# Focus

When people are in a terrible place in their lives it is important to listen to them deeply. Generally they will give clues to what is happening.

My friend John at church blew his brains out one Saturday morning a while back. He was a person that would never have admitted to depression or things not going right in his life. Yet everyone in church could see the sadness in his eyes, I believe. He was in a degrading and demoralizing marriage for which he and his wife had gone through counseling for years. He had a high stress job with increasing responsibilities. He had terrible money problems even though by anyone's standards he made a lot of money.

The official story was that his doctor had changed his depression medication and it had not had enough time to kick in yet. But as someone outside of his immediate family what I saw was a person that could not do anything about what was going on with him. He could not be really honest with anyone about what was tearing him up inside. I also think the focus of his life was on his job, other people, money problems so much so that there was little left inside him to care about the core of his being. The problems of his life got bigger than his soul and he crawled into the bedroom and shot himself.

As a friend I would have liked to have listened to him more, more about what was really going on with him. Had he indicated at all that he needed to talk to anyone? I think not. There were a group of people that would have met him for coffee any time of the day or night. Because no one really heard his pleas for help, no one helped. I think many of us could have been better clued in. That is all.

When the focus of our lives is on something or someone other than our own souls, we are in danger of losing our soul, the inherent place inside everyone of us that contains our eternal soul, our conscience, our self.

When we lose ourselves in relationships it is a process of giving up our selves to the relationship and losing something that is integral to our being and self preservation.

How can people be in long term relationships if they have lost their inner most self, yet this is sort of implied in "two become one" when they get married. I think when people are fully in love there has to be the deepest respect for the other person's soul or inner most being. I think that love must be part of becoming exactly who we are meant to become as individuals and as a couple.

In the very best of relationships I think there has to be some kind of reserving your soul for yourself in order to become exactly who you were meant to become. Keeping the focus of your life on you allows you save back a part of you that is integral to you being a unique human being on the planet, full of the potential for growth, expansion, living and growing into who you really are.

If you have given up your soul in a relationship, what will be left for you? This giving up of your soul can be the beginning of mental illness where you are separated from your Self. People who have lost their souls are not far from ending their lives because they believe they have no future.

The very most difficult thing about losing your Self in a relationship is that while you are damaging your soul, you are absolutely addicted to the exhilaration and excitement of it. If you are in this dangerous space, get help right away.

Getting and keeping the focus on your life is a coping skill that will allow you to continue to grow into who you are mean to be, identifying your mission on earth and fulfilling it. You can serve others best when you have the focus of your life on your self, so that you can give out of your wholeness. Selfishness is behavior that focuses only on you and your desires, making you incapable of seeing the needs of others and having empathy. Self-pity is focusing on what you lack and bemoaning it to anyone that will listen. Self-pity is feeling sorry for yourself that you do not have what you want and want to make certain everyone in your environment is miserable with you. Self-pity is based in lack of something which you feel you deserve but cannot obtain.

When you are in self-pity you are like a small child that is wailing for what it wants. It has no regard for others and has no emotional maturity to discern how to get the focus of their being on what is truly real and valuable in their life. A person in self- pity feels sorry for his or herself but would rather complaint and cry than to grow up and deal with the world as an adult.

A person who is deeply depressed and has a very active amount of self-pity going on can be in serious danger because they want what they want and will harm himself or herself if they do not get it right away. A person immersed in self- pity might need to be hospitalized in order the break the chains of what is going on in their mind.

Questions to journalize:

Is the focus of your life on you or someone or something else? How can you get the focus of your life back on you? What are your hopes, dreams, and goals? Start small if you need to.

_____

_____

_____

_____

What do you really like to do in your life?

_____

_____

_____

_____

What action steps can you take today?

_____

_____

_____

_____

If you find yourself in self-pity what do you do or what can you do to get out of it?

_____

_____

_____

_____

If you are in a period of selfishness, what do you do or what can you do to get out of it?

_____

_____

_____

_____

# Chapter 23

# Big & Little Things That Help.

This is a list of things I did to get well. These are little things and not so little things that over the long haul had a bigger impact on my life than I would have imagined possible. There are no "shoulds" on this list- it is meant only to give you some ideas of things that might help. You will be in a process of finding out what works best for you.

1.  I lived a life of routine. I went to work every day. I got up, cooked meals, cleaned house, did all of the super ordinary things of life. Sometimes I did them crying but I still did them. I inserted self help programs and therapist meetings as ordinary things I would do. The routine of it all was comforting in its own way. I tried to do nice little things too as part of my routine: a meal out with a friend, going to the public library or a movie, music somewhere. All of the things I did helped me to hang on to life.
2.  Journalize. I got a couple of pretty journals and kept notes on some things that I really wanted to do in my life.
3.  I journalized about my obsession in any way that I wanted to. Putting it on paper really gets it out of your life, slowly but surely.
4.  Slow down. Smell the coffee, the roses, and the rain. If your life is in frantic mode all the time you are stealing your own enjoyment of life. If you have kids take time to enjoy them as they grow up way too fast anyway. A close-call with death is an

opportunity to take stock and figure out where you are in your life. Slow down and enjoy the journey.

5. Learn how to procrastinate wisely. Figure out what you really want to do and love to do with your time and do that. Cut out things you hate to do. Others may be offended but brush them off, they will get over it.

6. Take any trip but a guilt trip. But don't fly off to Paris without telling anyone. No one wants to report you as a missing person. No one wants to worry themselves sick over you either.

7. I cried a lot. Crying, I believe, releases toxins from our bodies. It is the toxins that depress us on top of everything else that is going on.

8. To heal myself of my obsession on this man, I said a little mantra at work all day long to myself. I worked alone so no one overheard me. My mantra was, "I release you and set you free so that you may grow in all of the ways you need to." Saying this a lot helped me to forgive him and let go. In releasing him I was letting go of my resentment and fury at him for rejecting me. It helped.

9. I took a long camping trip with a friend. We camped from Ohio to the Olympic Peninsula in Washington State. We did this in May and the trip took a whole month. My friend returned from Seattle to go back to work and I went on to a Women's Commune outside of Grant's Pass, Oregon. I kept a journal of the whole trip as well as took dozens of photos to document my journey.

10. My trip to the commune was something I researched first which took my focus off the object of my obsession, and then got some recommendations from friends. At the commune I had my own little cabin on the side of a mountain. It was good to have my own space there where I could just be alone and cry if I needed to. They had some events, readings, circles that I participated in but I think what I really loved was just being alone in my own cabin on the side of the mountain. Oh and the food was totally natural and delicious. There are places for retreats all over the world. Find something that you want to do for yourself, something that speaks to your desires of what you want to do

to get well. It can be like summer camp for adults. Long term it can be a treasure that will live in your heart and encourage you.

11. The place where I took this retreat of sorts was a very safe place. The women there were very kind and understanding, listening to me when I chose to talk, not making any judgmental comments. It was a safe place where I could read and journalize, rest and enjoy the beauty of their mountain.

12. I learned everything I could about my SPIRITUAL SELF. I got closer to the God of my understanding more than I had ever done in my life.

13. As a Christian I believe the Holy Spirit lives within me. I think this time of healing is a matter of opening oneself up to the Holy Spirit and moving in our lives according to how the Holy Spirit moves us. I think too that if we listen better and deeper to the Holy Spirit, our deepest level of conscience as it were, we could stave off immense misery in our lives.

14. Sleep- I believe a nap in the afternoon or after lunch is a great thing to do for yourself. Even ten minutes of rest can revitalize you for the afternoon. I do not think that whole societies are wrong about this. Nor do I think that naps in kindergarten were for naught. However, if you are sleeping all day and all night, get it checked out. Excessive sleep, insomnia and sleep apnea are deeper medical problems. Get help on these.

15. Review the medications you are taking with your doctor or psychiatrist. Find out what side effects may be occurring that could potentially harm you. Seek out some alternative care if you like. I believe that holistic remedies, such as some tinctures and vitamins can have benefits but they are likely to be subtle and slow unlike pharmacology where results are rather quick on some meds, say within one or two weeks.

16. Foods-eat food that is good for you and stay away from highly processed unnatural foods. This alone can create some good changes in your emotions. Stay away from soda as every day we are learning how bad high fructose corn syrup is for everyone. On the other hand if you are an alcoholic, soda is better than alcohol. Use your wisdom on this.

17. I planted a few vegetables and flowers in the yard. Getting close to dirt helped me understand the cycles of life better. The

vegetables were good for me and the flowers took my mind off my obsession for a bit.

18. I went to the parks, for bicycle rides or rides out into the country. A change of scenery was just enough sometimes to get me out of my obsession.

19. I went to 12 step programs. 12 Step programs are completely anonymous and confidential It is the right of the individual to decide if they will disclose their own membership and participation. Suffice it to say that if you look them up in your phone book you will likely find one easily. There is a lot of healing within their walls and it is available to anyone with a problem related to the individual program.

20. I did not return to the church of my childhood but I did go see some people that I really loved from that time. I laughed and cried and prayed with some of them. It did my soul good to see them.

21. I took some college classes that I had always wanted to take.

22. I diverted my mind from the object of my obsession through reading, painting watercolors, photography and of course, journalizing.

23. I tried to have a new perspective about my life. What did I really want to do with my life? Where was I going? I had a job at the time that I absolutely hated which I eventually got out of and moved on to something I loved.

24. I got great counseling. I saw a psychologist once a week in the beginning and then every two weeks thereafter. She taught me about the focus of my life not being on me and why I was suffering physiologically from the void in the pit of my stomach. Learning all of this was not easy, only necessary.

25. I talked about what was going on with me with really close friends. I am certain they got sick of me but they never said so. They told me of similar experiences they had had and how they lived through them. They shared little tips that were marvelous for getting my mind off my obsession and onto my own life and future.

26. I sang a lot. All of that breathing has to be good for you. I sang with the radio, the stereo, in the shower, in my work vehicle. I sang everything from Country Western to Opera. Had anyone

seen me I am sure they would have thought me absolutely crazy. So it goes.

27. I listened to the life around me. Simple things gave me pleasure. Just having some patterns that I enjoyed in my life was very helpful. Listening to "Prairie Home Companion" every Saturday evening kept me grounded. It was a pattern I held onto for my very sanity and life. It helped.

28. I was not hospitalized. I had a strong support network of people I could call and talk to at a moment's notice. I hope that if someone felt I should have been hospitalized then I would have had the good grace to get myself checked in. Sometimes when people are suicidal they need to be taken out of their present environment for a while just to see things in a different light. Sometimes they need to be hospitalized to protect them from harming themselves. It is all part of getting well.

29. I made liberal use of the prayer lines, hotlines, crisis lines and I would call whenever I felt I needed to. I also got myself a sponsor in my 12 step program. This woman had a heart of gold and she listened to me when I needed it most. If she was busy she would say so and then get back to me later, but generally she would take time out in bits to listen to me. In the beginning I let it all pour out and each time we talked I talked way too long. As time went on I became clearer about what I needed and how much time I needed to talk. She was a godsend, a real pearl.

30. I learned to have some gratitude for my life as well. Keeping a gratitude journal has been a lifesaver for me too. I have heard that you cannot be miserable and grateful at the same time. Always a choice.

31. I had to learn about checking my motives. Why did I do certain things and was how I was doing things harming me? I used to want to please everyone I met. Now I do not do that. Sometimes I found myself lying to please others; not being truthful about things. If I find myself in a lie, I correct it immediately. It has given me tremendous freedom in my life. I have learned some coping skills that have helped me when I have found myself in a lie: saying to the person I lied to, "I need to correct what I just said to you." "I need to back the train up and correct what I just said." "Excuse me but I did not totally mean what I just

said . . ." This is a problem I no longer have because my coping skills have helped me change this aspect of my character. It is an immense blessing. I no longer have to say "I am fine" when I am not; I do not have to give my life's history but I do not have to brush away what I am really feeling either.

32. I had to change my perspective about my whole life, my loss and subsequent grief and I had to grow up and change my relationship to life itself. All good stuff.

33. Many programs and people suggest that in order to get outside of yourself the best thing you can do is help someone else. While I agree with this and I know this action to have value, I think there is a time when you must go into yourself and heal yourself first before you are well enough to reach out and help someone else. I think you will know when you are ready and the time is right.

34. However! I know a woman who lost her dog and husband within months of each other, and happened onto a job rocking babies at a daycare. She was immersed in her grief, was retired and needed something to do. She stopped by a daycare in her neighborhood and asked if she could come in a couple of days a week to rock babies. Not only could she do so but they wanted to pay her for it. So you have to decide for yourself what you want to do, how much you want to do, what, when, and where. And such activities are not set in stone. You can always change your mind later. She was a retired nurse so this was a special blessing for her.

35. Church- If you go to church, don't quit and if you want to find a new church, do so. Church is such a personal question that you really have to decide where you are on it. Some people cannot miss it and others go to the church of "Field and Stream" (hunting or fishing on Sunday mornings). Whatever works best for you is what is important. But be sure that a church that you decide to attend is a good fit for you-if if is not, run in the opposite direction. Churches can do a lot of damage to one's psyche if they are steeped in rules and hatred.

36. Organizations and Obligations- This is where you must get really honest with yourself. Do you really want to spend part of your life doing something you don't want to do? If you have to

streamline this part of your life do so. It is your life and your decision who you will give any part of it to. When you are in a healing process you get to decide. Some organizations are just not healthy for people if there is a lot of gossiping going on or busybody activities. What do you really want to do? Be assertive in this as it can really lighten your load.

37. Do something different. Do something that will change the course of your life, sometimes it is the smallest thing that has the greatest potential

38. Do as poets do- take a step back and take a deeper look at whatever. If something is holding you back from living the life you were intended to live, figure out how to change it, re-arrange it, and unload it.

39. However, if you need to get a divorce, or end your partnership relationship, group wisdom says to wait a year before doing so. You have so much to sort out at this time- hold off on huge leaps in your life until you are more at ease in your own skin. UNLESS!!! If you are in a relationship that is driving you to kill yourself, get out of it immediately. Go to a shelter, move into your parents' basement, put up a tent in a friend's yard whatever it takes. If you must get away from your spouse in order to protect your life, then you must do what you must do.

40. Stay away from toxic people. If you have someone in your life that harms you every time you talk to them, stay away from them. Getting well means getting rid of toxic relationships too.

41. Everything in life is change. Be prepared for it. Understand that others may not be ready for it as quickly or deeply as you are. Be kind with them and others. But after all is said and done, do change. For it is the changes we make today that may save our lives later.

42. While everything is change, if you smoke cigarettes or drink too much coffee, when you are in the healing process it is not yet time to go cold turkey. Give yourself some time. Get well first and then you can venture out into new territory.

43. Meditate or pray. However you choose to define your spiritual life is your business. But healing has to do with taking time out for your spiritual self. You can do something extremely simple in this regard or you can get tapes with music, guided

visualizations or readings. Find what you like best and make a commitment to yourself to do something every day even if only for a few minutes. I had a closet where I would go to pray, meditate, cry and sometimes scream at God. Whatever you need to do for yourself, do.

44. Read and write. I mentioned journalizing which I believe really helps but discovering what you like to read may give you material to journalize on. Be open to what others are reading and writing. I read a gazillion self-help books at this time. Some helped and when they did not help, I went on to the next one.

45. I did whatever it took to come back from the brink. I saw my journey as uniquely my own and that I was in a fight to save my life. I had lived through my suicide attempts and at a certain point I had fierceness about protecting my life from me. At that point, I then acquired tenacity about it too. It took a long time but I did it.

46. Life is precious. Do whatever you can to protect yours and the lives of your loved ones.

47. Learn some semantics, meanings of words, that will help you. Begin to understand how living a shame-based life can really hurt you inside. Give it up! Learn how to hand over guilt and shame to God.

48. I learned about creative visualization and did some exercises on a quasi-regular basis. One of my favorite visualizations is handing problems over to the hands of God. In 1983 I handed over cigarettes to God: 'I can no longer handle these, please take them and my addiction to them away from me for the rest of my life." I was ready to do this and it worked for me. I had tried everything else first. Creative visualization can be a good tool, but as in all things it is only a tool. You have to use it, learn about it fully and then use it.

49. At the beginning of your day, say a small prayer upon waking and then before you retire at night, go over your day and take your "inventory". This is a simple exercise but you will see yourself grow in tremendous and wonderful ways.

50. Learn to trust your "gut-level" feelings. When you feel something is really wrong with you don't wait to get help, get help immediately. There is no shame in admitting you need

some help or guidance through this. Better to ask for help than endanger your life and your future.

51. If you are a person of faith, trust the moving of the Holy Spirit in your life, or the focus of your worship. Tremendous lessons for our lives live within us, needing only to rise to our consciousness. Learn to listen to what is going on with you. You are worth it! This understanding may bring you tremendous blessing in your life.

52. Learn to "Wear the world like a loose garment." This was said to me years ago by an elderly woman who was a major blessing in my life. It means, to me anyway, to lighten up; we do not have to carry all of our problems and the problems of the world on our backs all the time.

53. Learn to "Take the next right step". This means that to the best of your ability, you put one foot in front of the other and move forward in your life. You do not have to have plans for the rest of your life at this exact moment; all you have to do is live your life for the next 10 minutes and then repeat. If you listen to what is going on inside you, you will discern a best path for your life.

54. Learn how to hand things over to your Higher Power. There is a time and a place to deal with certain things and what we cannot deal with we need to ask our higher power to deal with for us until we can.

55. Learn to frame life in a new perspective. You can train your brain to understand that tough times do not last forever. "This too shall pass." Or as Joel Osteen says, "It did not come to stay it came to pass". If you see tough times as temporary you can then grasp what you are meant to learn from them and get over them. Give yourself some time and space to learn this.

56. Read things that edify your soul. A good book can take you out of your misery while you read it. A good comedy can lift your spirits even if only for a while. Doing something to distract you is better than doing nothing at all.

Questions to journalize:

What are some little things that help you in your daily life? How can you put your attention on them and divert your thoughts from thoughts that harm you? What more can you do and what more do you want to do?

_____
_____
_____
_____
_____

What are some action steps you can take today?

_____
_____
_____
_____
_____

# Chapter 24

# Preventing Others From
# Harming Themselves.

In our desire to help others through this terrible time of life, here are
some ideas that might be helpful:

1. Be there for them, really be there. By this I mean that perhaps
   they need to have you physically close by for a while or maybe
   they need to know that you are truly listening to what they are
   saying.
2. Listen to them. Really hear what they are saying and not saying.
   What is their body language saying? So many people keep
   their suicidal ideation completely private but there are ways to
   understand better what is going on with them.
3. Just today a gal I work with told me of a friend of hers whose
   son committed suicide recently. She said it came totally out of
   the blue, a complete surprise.
   I think this is always possible for it to be a surprise but I would
   venture a guess that the son had been planning it for a long time
   but was so private about it that no one knew. Certainly this
   person must have given off some clues that he was not all right.
   We can never truly know what is going on inside someone but
   a mother knows better than anyone else when her child is sick
   and unable to tell her. Do you have a "gut level" feeling about
   someone? This feeling may be all that you are going to get from

this person. Best to start asking questions and checking it out. Also, I believe this "gut-level" feeling can be the moving of the Holy Spirit telling you to open your eyes, ears and heart to this person as they are in danger.

4.   The way we learn things in life is by making mistakes. Sometimes we are wrong if w try to second guess someone. Yet it is better to be wrong than sorry forever for not doing anything. Let go of the outcome of some of the mistakes you make. Making mistakes means that you are at least making efforts. Forgive yourself quickly for your "mistakes".

5.   If the person you love or care about is talking about suicide, call the police, the crisis line or your local hospital. Unless you are a licensed doctor, nurse, psychologist you may not know what is best to do. If the person needs to be hospitalized, step back and let the professionals do what they do best.

You can always apologize later if your actions were hasty but this is a situation Where failure to act can mean the loss of life. Better to err on the side of saving someone's life. Some discomfort on the part of your loved one is a small price to pay if they are in a suicidal episode at present.

7.   Cajole, harass, pick on the person you care about if you need to, to get them to get help. Drive them yourself. Go with them. This is not to be taken lightly.

8.   If your loved one has a gun, do not try to get it away from him or her unless you really know how. Call the police, they are trained to do this. You do not want to get killed in the act of trying to help someone else.

9.   If your loved one is violent, off their meds, or in some way threatening you, call 911 and do not try to deal with them yourself. If you try to take them to the hospital they could possibly harm you or others en-route or they could try to jump out of the car while it is moving. You may not be strong enough to handle them. Medical personnel are specially trained and will be able to subdue them. Don't risk your own life helping them.

10   A person in a psychotic or paranoid episode may be dangerous not only to themselves but to all around them. If they have a gun this increases the danger exponentially. Don't argue with them; just get the police to help as quickly as possible.

11. If you are caring for someone who is in a time of healing, do things with them. Go to a park; take the dog for a walk. Anything ordinary or routine, or somewhat special can really be a godsend.

Questions to Journalize:

What action steps can you take right now?

_____

_____

_____

_____

_____

Who can you call for help? You may need professional help to help get your loved one to professional help.

_____

_____

_____

_____

_____

# Chapter 25

# Talking Back To The Voices In Your Head

All of us have an inner voice or conscience that is talking to us all of the time. The question is what this inner voice is saying to us. If your inner voice is constantly berating you and putting you down then you need to change your inner voice.

This takes a lot of training but can be done. You have to seek out the positive voice within you and concentrate on what it is saying, and exclude from your senses the negative voice within. When you are in a negative phase you can talk your way out of it by learning some simple techniques.

I do this by taking time out to pray in my day. If I have a ton of crap floating around in my head, the negative voice becomes per-eminnent. It becomes immediately important to refuse to give it room or space in my head.

Through prayer and meditation, I go into that space and ask my higher power to help me get out of the negative space. I say things like, "I choose to change this situation for the better." "I am not a loser and the voice I hear saying this is not of God but of Satan." "I rebuke that voice." I choose to believe in myself, my future and my good life."

However you chose to talk back to the negative voice is up to you. The key is to develop your own list of sayings and affirmations and use them. They do help change the direction of your thinking. Gaining control over your own inner voice is a skill that can be of immense benefit to you and the loved ones in your life. To the degree that you learn this skill, your interior self will become stronger and your self esteem will improve.

Questions to Journalize:

Do you have a list of affirmations that you use regularly?

------------------------------------------------------------

------------------------------------------------------------

------------------------------------------------------------

------------------------------------------------------------

------------------------------------------------------------

Is anything holding you back from creating such a list? What action steps can you use to challenge yourself with regard to this skill? Can you put together a small list to start?

------------------------------------------------------------

------------------------------------------------------------

------------------------------------------------------------

------------------------------------------------------------

------------------------------------------------------------

# Chapter 26

# It Is Going To Take Time To Heal

A person that experiences suicidal ideation and thinks about it a lot is not going to heal overnight. It takes a good long while to get your SELF back and operating at good speed. Progress can be had every day by doing something that is beneficial for your soul something very simple that takes a bit of time and possibly some planning. Doing something is better than doing nothing. A walk, preparing a meal, washing dishes can take on a whole new meaning if you are doing these things to save your own life.

Adding something to your daily routine can really help. For several years I listened to "Prairie Home Companion" on public radio on Saturday evenings while I was cooking dinner and cleaning up afterward. This little routine got me out of the abject misery I was in even if only for a short time. The show was always charming and I remembered how to laugh a little and gained a new perspective on life.

Questions to Journalize:

What actions can you take today to nurture your soul?

_____
_____
_____
_____
_____

How can you take time out in your life for your healing?

_____
_____
_____
_____
_____

# Chapter 27

# Grief

Years ago I did some study on "Attachment Theory" that from before birth we are already in a cycle of attachment and separation from our mothers. Throughout our lives we are in a pattern of connecting to people and separating from them, siblings, friends, boyfriends and girlfriends, lovers, spouses, kids, grandparents, teachers of all kinds. To the degree that we continue to re-attach to life after separation situations, we are able to be resilient and well. We can also experience loss and separation from schools, jobs, careers, anything.

Grief is probably the most common of all human experiences and emotions. Grief simply is and can be a part of our lives over dozens of circumstances that are beyond our control.

Grief today though may come in the form of a loss of job, your 401K, your retirement plan. No matter what it is money is not a reason to kill yourself even though so many people see it as the only way out. Money is not a constant in our lives as it can change with the markets and the economy.

Grief can be deeply depressing, so much so that counseling is in order if you find yourself immersed in it. Again there are a multitude of options are available to get you some mental health.

When in Grief, it is very important to recognize it for what it is. Then you can understand the process of it, get help, and heal.

Grief is the body and mind's natural response to loss. In order to move forward in your life you have to say goodbye to the past. This is naturally very difficult to do for every person on the planet. However, to the degree that you say a good goodbye, you will progress in your healing process, in reattaching to life.

Separation theory says that we are always separating and reconnecting with everything in life. From the moment we are pushed out of our mother's womb we are in this dance of life where we connect to a person, place or thing and then through circumstances or aging, we lose them. Grief is the process of letting go of the relationship or whatever has been lost and then re-connecting with life through new relationships, new circumstances, new ways of living.

This is not just difficult it can be devastating. Bouncing back to life after a death, for instance, can take months and years. Couples who remain married for decades do not say goodbye easily when one of them passes away. But they, like everyone else must reconnect to life or cease growing.

Questions to Journalize:

Are you grieving a loss in your life? What is it and how are you dealing with it?

_____

_____

_____

_____

_____

# Chapter 28

# We All Have Only One Point

A concept that really helped me in my recovery plan was the idea that before God, we are all absolutely equal. Our value is exactly the same as everyone else's. We have only one point as do all other human beings on the planet. No person has more than one and no person has less than one.

Since we are all absolutely equal our responsibility to God is to become the very best self we can become, no more no less. We cannot compare our one point to anther's one point as we as individuals are completely different yet absolutely worth the same to God exactly as we are. We are meant to grow and develop into exactly who we were meant to be from before we were born, as we were "knit together in our mother's womb". Our value to God is to become exactly who we were meant to be.

Since our value to God is exactly the same, there is no use of comparing ourselves to others. If we are constantly comparing ourselves to others, we will assure ourselves that we will always come up short in many areas. This increases our negative feelings about our lives. It is freedom to release the need to compare ourselves to others. When we recognize that God sees us in all our special characteristics, exactly as we are, then we can grow to become exactly who we are meant to be, in complete wellness within ourselves.

I want to reiterate that it is pointless to compare ourselves to others. Our lives are different, our problems are different and our approaches to our lives are different. While we can take in new ideas or think about things differently, ultimately our approach to our own life is individual and unique.

Questions to journalize:

Do you ever find yourself comparing your life with someone else's?

_____
_____
_____
_____
_____

What can you do to stop this habit? What do you value about your own life?

_____
_____
_____
_____
_____

# Chapter 29

# Resentments And Getting Rid Of Them

"To Resent" is from the French verb, *Resentir* which means to feel again or re-feel, for us meaning to feel the pain of something over and over again. In AA we say that our resentments can kill us because if we live in them they will eventually cause us to drink again which could kill us.

If you have resentments boiling up inside you it is important to get rid of them. When you are immersed in the self-pity that resentments can cause you can become immobilized with grief, shame, hostility, and a dozen other emotions that may cause you to harm yourself.

It is important to develop the skill of isolating resentments in our heads, handing them over to our higher power and letting them go. However you get rid of them is up to you, the most important thing to do is get rid of them. I have heard that if you pray for someone you resent for two weeks, asking only for their good, the resentment will leave you. Forgive and forget, forgive, bury the hatchet and don't mark the spot where you buried it. Writing down your resentments and then burning the list also helps.

This is a skill that is learned over time. The result is that you will no longer feel resentment toward someone that harmed you in either a small or big way. Another little trick is to write it down on a small piece of paper and put it in a jar marked, "Things for God to do". Taking the problem out of your mind, putting it on paper and putting it somewhere for your higher power to deal with is a powerful exercise. If you check these notes months later you can actually see how things worked out to the good. Good stuff.

Questions to journalize:

Are you harboring resentments that are harming you? Make a list of them.

_____

_____

_____

_____

_____

How do you deal with your resentments. Do you know how to get rid of them?

_____

_____

_____

_____

_____

# Chapter 30

## Trusting The Process

When a person is in the process of healing themselves from suicide attempts they have to get themselves on a path that they can trust. Sometimes living day to day, putting one foot in front of the other, learning about yourself are enough. This protection of your SELF from yourself is a spiritual journey that is as unique as you are. No one else is exactly like you or has faced life in exactly the same way you have.

There is something wonderful about having the ability or teaching yourself to go deep within yourself for your own answers.

Someone once told me that"(Y)ou have to decide for yourself who you are". In this we are all in the same boat. Learning about your own mission on this planet, what piques your interest, what really awakens you to your life is what is important. So much is superfluous so that you really have to seek out what is most important to you.

Whether you are reading this book for yourself or to try and help someone you care about, I hope you get something that will help you in your journey. I hope I have encouraged you to get help or to help someone else get help. There is a lot of it out there and some of it is very good. If you get help that is not good, keep looking because good help is out there. You deserve it!

Questions to journalize:

Have you learned anything that will help you trust the process?

_____

_____

_____

_____

_____

Do find yourself trying to rush the process? How can you give yourself more time?

_____

_____

_____

_____

_____

# Chapter 31

# When All Goes Wrong . . .

I think every person on the planet has times when nothing seems to be going right and when it all seems to be going wrong. It seems like trouble comes in truckloads and is dumped on our doorsteps overwhelming us.

This is a matter of perspective. Perhaps what looks terrible to you may be the opening of a doorway into your life that you never imagined though desired with your whole heart. Certainly this is not new news; certainly someone told you this at some point in your life. But do you believe it; deep in your soul believe it?

I think it is time to step back and seek the deeper answers. What is going right in your life right now? Is everything going wrong or seemingly only most of it? It would be like having your doctor tell you you have cancer on the day your spouse asks for a divorce. Can things get worse? Yes they can, you could end it all by killing yourself. People go through hard times and survive; they pick up the pieces strewn about like so much garbage and they move on.

My community suffered the worst flood of our history in 2008. The flood wiped out hundreds of homes and businesses. The heartbreak was not losing the house because houses can be replaced. The heartbreak was losing the photographs and mementos that could not be replaced. But when you have your life you can always start over. We were so blessed that no one lost their life in the flood of 2008. There were millions and millions of dollars worth of damage but no one died. People were forced to evacuate and they did.

I worked with a gal who lived in our Czech Village community, a little historic enclave of homes and businesses built here by the first settlers over 150 years ago. She had been born in her house, grew up in it, inherited it when her mother and father passed away, raised her children in it, retired in it and I think thought she would die in it too. She had lived there for 80 plus years. Her daughter described the wreckage: "It was as if everything had been tossed about like in a washing machine's centrifugal force. Everything was broken and filthy and tossed against the opposite walls by the force of the water." It was horrendous and she lost virtually everything.

But her strength of character even at 80 years old was so strong. She and her son moved themselves first into a FEMA trailer, then into an apartment and started acquiring the things they needed through gifts from churches and other groups. They survived the FEMA trailer until they could find someplace else.

There are people who face adversity with such grace and strength they are an inspiration to us all. I want to be like her.

Resilience in life is a great gift. May you be blessed with an abundance of it.

God Bless You and Protect You on Your Journey through this life.

Questions to Journalize:

Have you learned anything new you can use for yourself?

_____
_____
_____
_____
_____

Have you learned anything you can use with someone else?

_____
_____
_____
_____
_____

# Chapter 32

# "The Land Of Beginning Again"

When a person attempts suicide and survives they are in a special place in their life. All at once they see that they very well could have succeeded in their attempt. If they have any sense of the value of life they can then see that they have been given another chance to live. They are "above the dirt". Each day can be viewed from a new perspective-asking "What can I do with my life today?" "What is my purpose on this planet today?" "What can I do for me to get well?" "What is wrong with me and my life and how do I change it for my good and the good of those who I care about and who care about me?" This is not easy by any stretch of the imagination, only necessary.

When you survive a suicide attempt, you can then get through your depression, embarrassment, and guilt which can happen with good care. You can see yourself in the "Land of Beginning Again" where you have an opportunity to pick yourself up, brush yourself off and get back on the bicycle or horse and attempt to ride again.

So many of us have tremendous guilt and shame after attempting suicide. We have to get enough help so that we are not guilt and shame based. We have to become strong enough in and of ourselves to never attempt it again; we have learned our lesson that we really can face anything in life and survive.

There will come a time when we will meet our maker, let us not try and control that date ourselves. Our duty to God is to live out our lives to the best of our abilities, to discover who we are and why we are here. It is up to us to find our own path and proceed on it.

You are worth it! Best wishes to you on your journey through life.